Matthew John Borkowski died on April 15th, 2017.
He was 65 years old. He passed away peacefully
sitting on a bench on George Street, in downtown
New Brunswick, NJ, a city he lived in most of (but
not all of) his life. This booklet of Matt's poetry was
put together for a Memorial Poetry Reading in his
honor. A much larger Collected Poems is in the
works & is forthcoming from Iniquity Press.

Some of the poems in *THE REINCARNATION OF SHELLEY
And Other Poems* have appeared in Matt's first book *UPTOWN DOWN!*
& in several small press poetry magazines including: Arbella, Ball Peen,
Bee Hive, Big Hammer, Half Dozen of the Other, Long Shot, Lummox,
Street Value & online at outlawpoetry(dot)com

Front cover collage by Michael Shores
Design/layout: Angela Mark

Iniquity Press/Vendetta Books
are edited by Dave Roskos
at POB 906, Island Heights NJ 08732-0906

Contents

A Walk is a Prayer   1

The Father in the Hallow Moon   2

When Angels Die   3

The Reincarnation of Shelley   4

Guillotine   5

What End Of The Whip Are You On?   6

Cold Rock River   7

After Reading Spengler (in the toilet)   8

Late   9

A Most Erudite Man   12

Luck   13

Sunday at the Homeless Shelter   14

Haiku (crescent moon)   17

I Wanna Win   18

Golem   23

Why Poets Commit Suicide   28

Kongorikishi   29

Eunuch #1217   30

Ashtoreth   31

Pride   32

For Mary's Hair   33

Incongruous Flood of the Hydra Laws   34

The Broken Violin   35

Christmas 2012   36

Who Loves The Little Fish?   37

A Walk Is A Prayer

a walk is a prayer if taken well,
one foot in heaven,
one in hell;

upon the earth where all have fallen,
a walk is a prayer

The Father in the Hallow Moon

the father in the hallow moon
swooning sins upon the harp,
in monocles and follicles
he weaves the web that guides the heart.

rather a demon glazed in frost,
with fast foot thunder on the run,
than patient logic, neatly coursed,
to lead a life that's never won.

the father's arm is wisdom's aim,
it rests upon a throne,
and when it rises through the air
the gutter calls the vagrant home.

When Angels Die

time and it's headstone misplaced on a mantle,
destroying even the taste of words;
these are the things that form the tomb.

these are the things: their monuments rotted;
asking not even their fallen king,
for one last silent sigh.

there are such things as ghosts in alleys
and blazing stars that fail to shine.
there are such things: the frail and tragic--
things of beauty, lost and lame.

Over moons and cracked windows, the mongrel sun
hangs dumb; and silence seeks shelter beneath its shade,

destroying even fleshy ghosts within its web of flame

These are the things! (all poets cry)
For silence sings when angels die

THE REINCARNATION OF SHELLEY

the reincarnation of Shelley pumps gas on
    the corner of Commercial and Handy,

    blows his credibility at the foodstamp office,

    tries to cut his wrist in a public toilet,
    fails; and calls collect Miami--an old girlfriend
    won't accept the charges

    "I'm too good," he thinks to himself, "too good
    for my own good, that's what's gonna kill me."
    etc., and next life I'll probably come back as a
    backgammon set, near someone's swimming pool, and then
    they'll appreciate me, I bet....................

the reincarnation of Shelley says weird things, like--
    "a cigarette...one cigarette...can keep you from
    losing your mind"...
    jailhouse talk, ya know?...and
the reincarnation of Shelley has never even been to jail,

    but he's pissed...he relates to Black men
    in cages,
    has read LeRoi Jones,
    thinks Hinkley should be canonized,

the reincarnation of Shelley is a sick dude,
    but he knows it,
    wears a cross now, too,
    no more atheist shit,

oh no,

but he isn't mellow either,
bet your ass he's angry,

"regular or unleaded," he hisses, when
you drive in,

"and pull up a little,
I can't reach the tank..."

GUILLOTINE

I carved initials in stained glass
    they ran like blood in flame
your arm
        an act of avarice
    a joke upon the plate

they stunk like burning rubber
    I saw each street a gutter
    and prayed to saints in agony
        to have my eyes removed

    your parasol through windows crawl
to hunchbacked children
                stuck in stalls
to which all the rejected call
    to spit upon your gate

WHAT END OF THE WHIP ARE YOU ON?

what end of THE WHIP are you on?
in the collective morality
con.
lash centrifugal,
handle home,
sun drenched pavements
contribute

nothing.

what end of THE WHIP are you on?
security junkie faun?
baby blue metal charioteer?

what end of THE WHIP are you on?
      (the handle doesn't feel the heat,
   the weight
        of the
        LASH,
          the
        GASH   IT
          RIPS   the
     backs of
        tear-soaked concubines, who sew
    your bloody   shoes.
what end of THE WHIP are you on?
in the HUGE MORALITY CON!!!!!
for what end were you groomed and tuned and
trained?

the handle world's a home,
the RIP of the LASH,
its
    GASH,
        only the
OUTSIDE
    knows;
        what end of THE WHIP are you on?

THE COLD ROCK RIVER
of broken glass
    starts dark struck wind
    becoming stronger

    On State Street
    Dostoevsky kicks old ladies

    mules die too

    and after six the town folds
all but for the river
        and fat cops
    who eye holy whores
        and hair cream
    Lolita smiles
       to think back now
       how she knew Nietzsche
       in an alley

After Reading Spengler (in the toilet)

old spring is hung round the necks of whales
paint the flabby underbellies,
long the thin manes of cancerous giraffe,
stones of Germanic philosophy;

give us a new equation!

most people are fast to oblige
most people don't believe the real
world has anything
to do
with itself anymore;

Lincoln's just the head on the penny,

hippopotamus dribble,
the old, old infamy,   another holiday.

spit and more spit
                    Most people don't care to
see the world   with it's tongue stuck   out,
                    it's eyes rolling,
    it's nose twitch twitching sneezing   yellow
pus.

                    PROXIMITY,   is everything.

      face the facts.
shred the Christmas new year with
the axe of the decimal, spark the tree limb once again.

HISTORY IS SOUL IN PROGRESS, the weight of chains
on dead martyrs, whose names we can't even recall,

balloon men all, spiked with vomit drums, they beat,
BEAT BEAT   old blood for new sacraments

Late

the world was created in fifteen minutes,
the same time it will
take for the bus I am
waiting for to
arrive.

yes, fifteen minutes.

a unicorn with broken teeth
told me this dreadful truth
one time near a
lilly pad as
I sat detoxing
from despair.

The bus I am waiting for took longer to make.
It was made by
greasy men with
greasy hands most of whom
hated their jobs,
but did it anyway
cause they like
to eat.

they did not know me,
and they did not know
someday i would be
waiting for something they made;

it's always that way.

Their effect on my life has been
monumental;

their bus is an instrument
of exquisite torture,
and it
may be late.

Ever since the world was first
created (in fifteen minutes)
lateness has been a
constant factor in
man's development.

Lateness has contributed to
more misery than possibly
any aspect of
our existence, other
than maybe Greed and
Fear.

when terrible things happen they
are always on time;

but when things
are late,

well,
we can only
wonder,

and wait

a certain wisdom

I watched her ass move
down the street, and thought
to myself,
there's a certain wisdom in the way she moves

that'll make a man work all week long.

Hispanic,
19,
black patent leather pants, tight
red blouse,
white heels six inches high;

with short Pat Benatar hair, and
eyes and lips pouting.

I watched 3 dudes walk up to her,
and follow her along
down the street.

She's the prize
in a world
they'll never get out of.

19,
firm tits,
in her tight black pants
and white
stiletto heels,

yeah, that's somethin' a man'll work all week for;
an' to have a son he can name Miguel, after his grandpa,
an' have a blue Pontiac convertible
with fuzzy dice hangin'
from the mirror.

An' I watched her move
on down the street, with
her 3 suitors,
these Hispanic dudes,
an' i thought how these three guys probably all work
together in some recycling plant in Fords or South Amboy,
where people bring old books and newspapers,
an' they grind em' into pulp,
an' make cardboard out of em', an' paper bags for the
super market,
an' I thought, ya know,

there's a certain wisdom in
that
too

a most erudite man

After drinking all night
with Edgar Poe,
I decided to take his advice--

I'll never write about talking birds.

Luck

God is luck to the luckless,
God is a bartender in the Bronx without any teeth

only people w/ no luck
really know luck,

only those behind the fence
know the distance,

only people who hate God need Him or Her or It.

God is the Ace of Spades,
just before it
slams you.

I'm worried about God,

the luck the poor don't have,

the rotting breasts of light
glimpsed through the
window

SUNDAY AT THE HOMELESS SHELTER

If Christ came back
we'd kill him again
this morning
but he won't, so we can't.

and the staff is asleep,
and there's a child somewhere,
but not here;

here is failure personified on
40 bunk beds,
clothing from the Goodwill Mission
stuffed in crates underneath and
then some hanging limply drying
from the steam pipes.

there are many geniuses here
with me in the homeless shelter,
and many more sleeping
under bridges
and on subway grates;

a genius is a person who
will not compromise their opinion.

we know we are right.
Amen.

at night when all us geniuses
are sleeping, the fumes of
our thoughts climb towers
to our dreams,
and although our bodies are buried in
exhaust and humiliation,
we know we are right,
and time is a liar.

time is just a fat roach
to be crushed at tomorrow's
breakfast table, if we can
find one;

time is just a sweet little
blackhead on our noble cheeks,
to be squeezed and wiped
when the spirit moves us.

time is a liar.

we're not afraid of time; killing time is as easy as taking
a piss, an' cheaper, too;
the other geniuses and I know
the essence of time,
we know how to split a match
in half, and how to brush
our teeth with salt,
and how to make a dollar
last a whole day and then some....

an' how to roll a cigarette with one hand,
an' when to fight and when
to speak,
and when not to fight and when
not to speak,
and when to flush the toilet,
an' when not to flush the toilet,

the other geniuses and I are
DANGEROUS! --

no folks,
Einstein was not a genius.

he was just a fat little kid
with crazy hair--who excelled at something he
didn't really understand,

he'd never survive down here.

we'd squash him like a beetle
and watch his guts ooze out
his asshole--

no more gardens in Princeton,
no more atom bombs either;

we'd steal his tomatoes and
smash them in the street;
so much for relativity!

cause we know we are right,
and time....
well,

what time is it in Nagasaki?
don't know huh?

don't care either?

time is a cat with its eyes gouged out,
a bottle of cheap wine sucked down through
the phlegm of another day's
mercy killings;

we could care less if the whole damn machine
blew up right now, spitting blood and
smoke
through these halls of hell,

we'd laugh,
bum another cigarette, an' maybe then,
wash out our socks and hang 'em
on the heat pipes,
for tomorrow.

so much for tomorrow

tomorrow--should it come--
will find us as we are
today--

content in our anger,

and not quite dead
enough
to
rise

Haiku

crescent moon
swims circular
as if
some

falling
God
could walk upon
it

I WANNA WIN

What happened?
I wanted to be an
artist--a great artist.

I wanted to continue the
work that Christ had
started, change the
world, all that; --

But here I find
myself in a McDonalds
playing their Million Dollar
Monopoly Game--
and
I wanna win.

All I need is piece #53
and I get a $1000 dollar
shopping spree at Sears

          What the hell, --
What would I buy?

What would Christ buy?
or Jackson Pollock?

What would Emily
Dickinson buy on
her shopping spree,

underwear and envelopes?
a black veil?

Does Sears carry black
veils?
probably only through
their catalog service.

What would Hart Crane
purchase?

an erector set and
a deck of tarot cards?
a flower pot for Pocahontas?

Bukowski'd get a power
drill and 4 dozen
pair of stockings to
give out to his broads,

Christ would give it
all away
warning them never
to eat Egg McMuffins
ever again

Verily, Verily

Whitman would buy
$800 worth of first
aid cream and bandages
and a Greyhound
ticket to Gettysburg,

But me, what would I
get with the
$1000?

Ah, I ain't in a
class with any of
those guys,
I've less compassion
and less talent too,
a lot less
I'd probably get a VCR--
and some dresses for my daughters,

I've got as much
guilt as Kafka

What would Poe
buy?

Does Sears carry coffins?

Ginsberg would get a
bunch of mattresses
and lay them
on the railroad tracks
protesting
plutonium

Kerouac'd get
a nap sack & sleeping
bag, & plaid flannel
shirts, all red &
a case of gallow burgundy

Halliday would spend
it all on colored pencils
and crayons.

Corso'd shoot it up,
and if Burroughs won
he'd cut it
up.

They say Hemingway
couldn't get it up,
but if he won he'd
probably hit
the sporting goods dept.

Frost would buy a shovel,
snow boots and a scarf

Pound would buy a ham radio

But what would I
buy?

Damn, a whole
thousand dollars
I could get a new stereo,
yeah and every Madonna
album ever, a Madonna poster--sure,
a CD player, and
Cowboy boots,
a Swiss army knife w/ 86 blades

and a telescope--
a chainsaw, yeah -- I
could start my own business

nah, I'm too lazy--they
would only go to rust

Anyway, I don't think
I'm gonna win,
nope, not a chance,

I just drank 5 cups
of coffee and every time I
get a game piece, it's one
I already have, in triplicate

Well, at least I'm not
drunk--not today anyway

What would
Dylan Thomas buy?
Does Sears sell
stomach pumps?

GOLEM

clay wedding figure
straddles yellow line
three ton flame follows
Golem home

seeking some vanishing point
the crack under the door shouldn't admit light
but it does,

news from the bureau hasn't been good,

but Golem denies it,

the company needs a new trademark, can't move
enough people with the old one;

so Golem sends 40 tons of bananas overseas to
compensate,
and curses the gamble, but what can he do?
it's sink or swim,
damns the old emblem, it's silly colors

Golem Tuesday Morning

Golem brushes his teeth, shines his shoes
factories out like a thick law journal praising progress,
every creed wilts celebration under Golem,

who makes dog food out of their hands and feet
sending helium balloons to the survivors

Golem Wednesday 2:17 P.M.

Golem goes to the dentist, mumbling "forgiveness is formlessness"
his dentist agrees, and tells him to dig the Tchaikovsky tape in
the elevator,
newsboy in wheelchair stares at Golem as he leaves

23

Golem feels compassion, not pity,
they should build more ramps, he thinks,
that's the way to go.

Golem Friday in the Warehouse

perusing the white lines,
he likes what he sees, the neat rowed boxes
stacked on pallets filled with severed heads
waiting for shipment should bring a good price,
yes.

Golem adjusts his flag pin,
runs his thumbnail
down his
red vest,

Golem is pleased, he will tell Mrs. Golem tonight over dinner,
they may be able to afford
the summer home in the Hamptons,
after all,

Golem turns aside,
away from the WORLD,

touches the soft aching flesh of his
prick through the hole in his pocket.

Monday is Golem's birthday, he's accomplished
much in his 43 years,

more than most
Golems,
and he never stumbled,
never faltered,

and most important,

this Golem ALWAYS KEPT IT CLEAN,

what the personal cost and aggravation....
and it hasn't been easy.

CLEAN GOLEM.

that's the miracle.

Golem at Work, Golem at Play

Golem at a softball game,
Golem and more Golem.

Golem in the mountains,
Golem fishing in the sea,
Golem at a party,
Golem drinking tea,
Golem with new shoes,
Golem in sweat pants,
Golem naked
his right foot in the air,
Golem in the barber's chair.

Golem this and Golem that,
Golem.

Golem addressing a group of younger, yet rising
Golems,
Golem on a train platform,
the New York Times folded neatly under his arm,

Golem, in a lawnchair
sipping an ice cold beer,

Golem driving Mrs. Golem to her Aerobics class.

Golem alone.

Golem with Golem junior.

Golem drunk on New Year's Eve singing
"should old acquaintance be forgot!"
Golem sick on New Year's Day.
Golem yelling through the football game,
"Come on, COME ON!," pounding his fists
on the table,
Golem excited.

the many, many moods of Golem.

Golem visiting his dying father in the hospital
saying, "don't worry, you'll be O.K."
Golem lying.
Golem thinking, well, it's not the end of the world.
even the end of the world isn't the end of the world
to Golem.

Golem in despair,
Golem feigning charity.

Golem angry at the traffic
Golem, on the telephone complaining about
prices,

Golem greeting other Golems at a small gathering,
Golems everywhere.

Golem likes himself and other Golems,
or at least he tries to, that's the kind of
Golem he is.

kind Golem,
patient Golem,

and most important,
CLEAN GOLEM

Golem voting for his favorite candidate on November 5th,
Golem happy when his candidate wins,
Golem not surprised,
Golem says the tide has turned,
Golem knows things will get much better now.

Golem believes his country is the GREATEST COUNTRY IN
THE WHOLE WORLD!!!!!
Golem believes in freedom,
Golem sorry other Golems in other countries aren't
free like him,

Golem loves his freedom.

Freedom to be the kind of Golem he wants to be,
freedom to watch any show he wants on television,
freedom to read anything his Golem heart desires,
freedom to buy any kind of car he wants and finance it
through any bank he wants, with any type of payment plan
he wants

freedom to drink any brand of soft drink he chooses,
anytime he chooses,
freedom not to drink soft drinks, freedom to say
fuck soft drinks, fuck all soft drinks,
I'll just drink water, Thank You.....

Golem thinks we should free the entire globe,
even if we have to use force,
even if we have to kill a lot of people in the
process.....they'll thank us for it
eventually,

yes,
Golem and Mrs. Golem agree,

it's damn nice
being free

Why Poets Commit Suicide

the worst people in the world,
become poets,
why?

to wring the worm in their soul?

probably,
anyway I'd rather hear a banjo anytime

I'm selfish

I wanna put God in a drawer,
away from everybody,
like
a gold
watch.

Why do poets commit suicide?
Why does anybody commit suicide?

cause they can't take it anymore,
that's why.

can't take what?

themselves.

the worst people become poets,

crying for an audience,
want to be loved,
all that.

it's not worth it,
wanting to be loved,

it never works.

any ass on the corner will tell you--

that's why poets commit suicide

KONGORIKISHI

grey stone serpent
                    flowered death
        the deep carved idol's eyes

is hell or vengeance in that wrath
        or love transformed by hate's disguise?

Jahweh holds the flaming sword--
        what lies beyond the gate?

        the image of the mirror's front,

        reversed to
        contemplate

EUNUCH #1217

said poor Jeremy
9 years old

in 1376 A.D.

being led to
minor surgery

"But Your Worship,

I don't care to sing
like an
Angel!"

Ashtoreth

why piss in the sink?--when
Ashtoreth is holding her Oriental
robin,

as a rose caresses the floor.

Is nothing sacred in this dream we
call our burden?

    -a bouquet of telephones
            wire the latest crucifixion on a
dare,
    her face,
           her vase,
      so pale,
           no moon,
     three swans;

a faint outline next to the bureau.

she never moves, never winks,
  our urine is
rain   and
foolish

starts;

and vanity,
vanity,

in her arms

the world a sad toy,

two spiders mate on the
crease of her gown,

another nation falls to
ruin,

as you turn the faucet closed
again

Pride

Pride stroked the long of
the serpent's plumes,

the concrete maze of business sense,

broke the bells and broke the children,
broke the leaning of the fence;

Pride cracked the dry bone,
the furied sea,
the ram's horn,
the dumb sound,
the bird's wing,
the fish fin,
the lute string;

Pride buried half the world,
and the other half
we don't know,

Ah, the sting of moon glow!

for Mary's Hair

when a cloud breaks,
when a wave parts,
when a storm brews
over crests of sky;

when a dream aches,
when the sea roars,
when a gull dives
through the cold air;

when a child cries
in her mother's arms;
when the wheel turns
in the playground,

are her feelings hurt?
are her tears dry?

when a song smiles
in a hot sun,
when the sound laughs
like a big drum;

when it falls
on her shoulders,

are her plans done?

The incongruous flood of the hydra laws

The incongruous flood of the hydra laws
ruined the fisherman's holiday,
and left all the whales on the beaches
without even so much as
a word to say!

In keeping with Octopus' dreams of clay
and bloodbaths that washed all their
plans away!

Past elections were all ruled invalid,
and the dictator sharks
given mastery

* * * * * * * * * * * * *

delicate porpoise dichotomies
   trace the wear on an old Roman coin,
   Medusa's head yawns and flies over
   the map of a coast she destroyed;

a bomb is sewn into the carpet of a hall
   where an Emperor kneels,
   breaking the backs of his children
   whose torture is always concealed.

The Broken Violin

love falls
from the ceiling lights
around my broken violin,

Billie Holiday picks it up
And walks it over to the window.

"You play this thing?" she asks.

"Yeah," I said, "I used to, till it broke.
I threw it against the wall."

"Reminds me of that cat you once
had," she says, "the one you loved but was
never yours,....what ever happened to that
cat?"

"I don't know," I say.

"You want some dope?" she asks,
"I got some good shit!"

"No,...it doesn't help anymore. It doesn't work,.."

"So you realized?"

"Realized what?"

"That you can't own anybody,...you can only love them..."

"Yeah, I don't own anything,...."

"Yes you do!"

"Yeah,..what?"

"You own the broken violin!"

Christmas 2012

Truth--that two edged
sword fell down
somewhere between
George Washington's horse
and Einstein's head
behind Palmer Square

Reality's like Play Dough, isn't it?
bend it, pull it, shape it into any size,

and Christmas came so fast this year,
some people almost missed it,

pondering dead 6 year olds,
and NRA Romneys hanging
cliffs of cold delirium,
the Maya end
maybe 4 months off;

and - "it's not that I'm afraid to die, ... I just don't
wanna be there when it happens"
(Woody Allen)
everybody's getting older
Mick Jagger looks like Don Knots;

and yet, ... there's a place somewhere,
somewhere .. far, far away, ...
that's not controlled by the cartoon media,

where Christ really
died,
and we
were
saved

Who loves the little fish?

the big fish eats the little fish
powered by legality,
a power false but driven by the
pardon of the world.

the world it grows upon
crab claws as decades
roll and yawn,

amoebas climb the surface scrolls that
line our yellowed walls;

the Spirit, though, it still believes in truth,
(the Rising Tide!),
and loves the little fish the most,
who swam and rode,
and died

Made in the USA
Middletown, DE
26 March 2021